To Rowan

The Way Out

Kate North

So sorry you couldn't make the reading!

Kate
Oct 2022

PARTHIAN

Parthian, Cardigan SA43 1ED www.parthianbooks.com
First published in 2018
© Kate North 2018
ISBN 978-1-912109-46-3
Editor: Susie Wild
Cover design by Torben Schacht
Typeset by Alison Evans
Printed in EU by Pulsio SARL
Published with the financial support of the Welsh Books Council
British Library Cataloguing in Publication Data
A cataloguing record for this book is available from the British Library.

For George

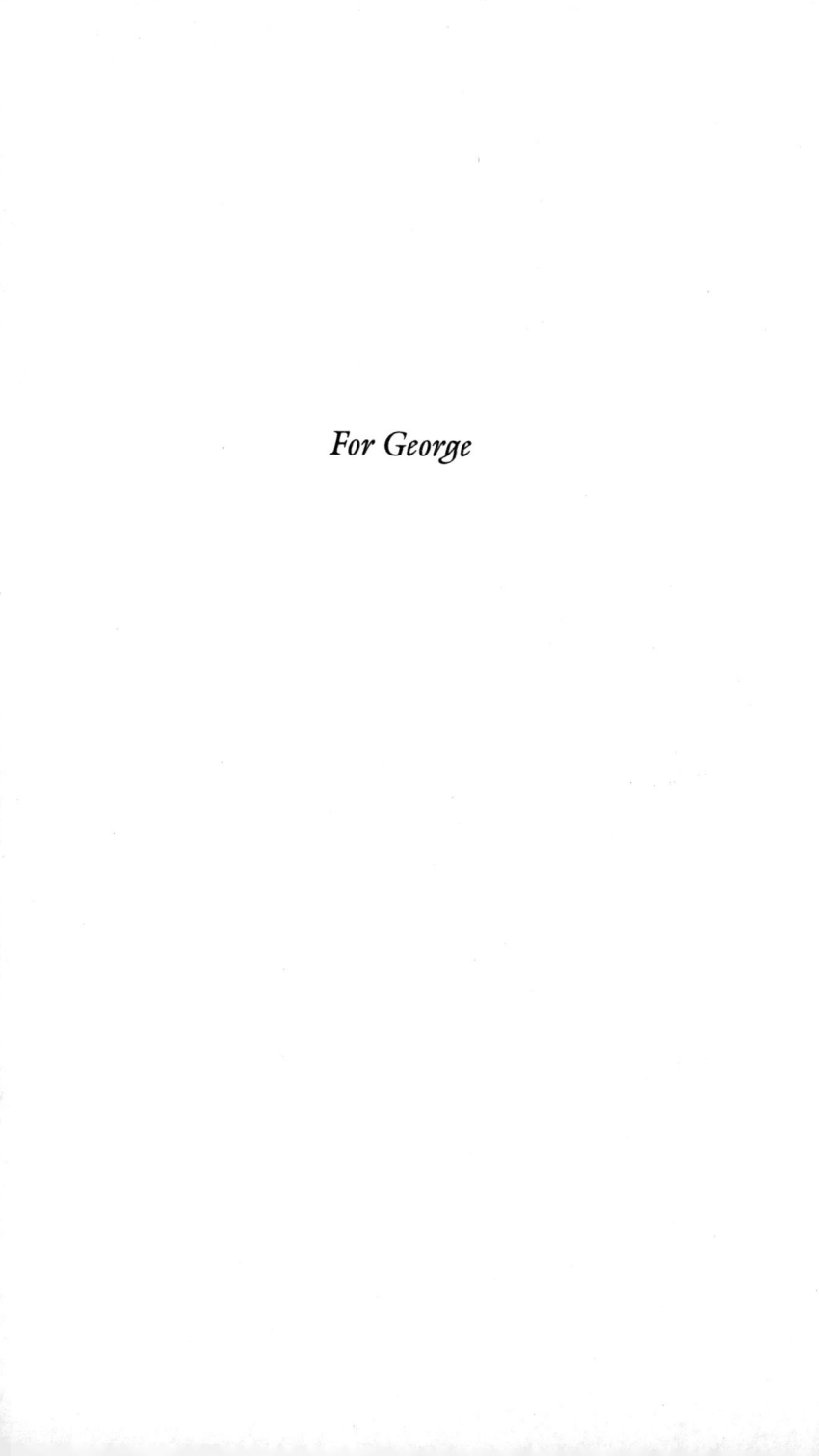

Contents

In

Entrances	1
Lighting the Fire	2
Enhanced Care Unit	3
Target Treatment	4
Spleen	6
Liver	7
Kidneys	8
Lungs	9
Pancreas	10
Heart	11
Hematocyte	13
Grand-Mary	14
At The Sink	15
Le Café Mollien, Musée du Louvre	16

Through

Taff End	19
Under the Heath	20
NATO, 2014	22
Sunderland	24
The Way to the Hide	25
The Way from the Hide	26
Murmuration at Manorbier	27
Outside In	29
Paris, December 25th	30
Vasa	32
Lucilia Sericata	34
An A to Z of Saints	35
Going Feral	36
The Process	37
Bridges I Have Known	39

Out

The Way Out	43
Fix	44
Parks	45
Skin	46
Edgelands	47
Under the Weather	48
Cathays Cemetery	49
Asti, Balcone	50
Tours, Jardin	51
Roath, Garden	52
St George's Castle	53
Port El Kantaoui	54
Rumspringa at the Lake	56
Mount Ainos	57
Signal at Banceithein	58
Notes on the Poems	61
Acknowledgements	63

In

Entrances

Whether you leap into the world a frog prince
               fall out of your mother a birthed foal
               wheel through the door a spooling thread
               reach the window as a fire-fighter,

your way in won't show you
how to cross the road, gliding
like the jay or using the pelican,
how to eat the apple, seeds and core
or quartered with a knife, how to kiss,
open mouthed or nipping like a mouse.

You can see the world
in monochrome or technicolor;
choose to deseed the chilli or not.

Lighting the Fire

After summer we're out of practice,
the kindling pyre collapses,
we burn through lighters
double pace, it can take three
attempts before flame catches
fuel in its warm lick.

Radiators tick their support,
blankets litter the sofa,
we double-up on socks and the cat
renews his friendship visa.

Returning from the world
through our hot wall
I open the door to you,
pillow heavy, cheeks
blooming like poinsettia.

Evenings measure the burn
and grow with ember,
our routine becomes neural
with each morning sweep,
every coal delivery, until the flare
is summoned with a finger snap,
skill sharp flint, instinct set like a fossil.

Enhanced Care Unit

Shape of a woman

                hung like cloth

in a sauna. Five souls, a standing

                      circle around her.

She's so small

    tiny.

A not silence, broken breath
                      between us.

Her hands an obscure fact

that will keep crashing back, in the shower, tying a lace,

               at the wheel and against cheeks.

Hold,

    siblings intertwined,
        wet skin on skin,

then the rack-stack rigidity, Russian dolls descending

               in awkward acquaintance,

mice to owls.

Target Treatment

I had not touched you before,
you were sat on the corner
of your father's bed, tear-clogged
and dumb, shaking head.

When you saw me you lied
a smile, shifted your weight
then waved. The sudden retreat
before us, grasping, grasping
and clutching the air.

You had never seen anyone look this old,
never heard the nursery gurgle
nor tried to match the distanced stare.

If you want him to eat

                feed him.

                The decline is rapid.

We can tell you more

                after the weekend.

He has been hiding food.

                We don't have his records.

You pierced the foil lid
and pushed down, unsure
of the routine. *Da, Da, Dad,
good, good, good. I'll call Mam
to bring you some more.*

In the lift we shook our heads,

>then in the A&E cul-de-sac
>we stood, we sighed, we hugged.

It was hot and I can still recall
the damp of your neck, your back.

Spleen

Between the ribs
old red cells filter
into the iron reserve
with a white pulp centre.

This compassionate activity:
recycling sad laughter,
angry bacteria removed.

Liver

You are my winter
                red breakdown
                              raising blood,
jealous transport
                vital anger store,
                              greedy infection
                              strategic object of desire,
            scarred Titan divining
power, enlarged wrath,
vulnerable growth supporting

toxic regeneration,
my woman, my courage.

Kidneys

Blood stones
high in the cavity
either side of your spine,
tough tissue
at oblique angles,
capsule filters
concentrating waste.

A passive counter-current
regulating good and evil,
conscience and reflection
maintaining your acid-base.

Paired cysts burned
at the altar, offered
in a meat pie, judged
beans on scales
determining your health.

Lungs

Shock triggers our first breath,
in seconds we contract,

fluid absorbs speech made real
through exchange within our cave.

Fraternal twins
our walls slide frictionless,

with cardiac impression,
the rib-marked surface.

We strain through negative
pressure, a vital capacity

to draw in, pump out,
relax.

Pancreas

Head, neck, body, tail,
buds rotate,
fuse.

Whole flesh secrets
 α, β, δ, γ,
circulate.

Well-marked prominence,
blood branches,
juice drains.

Groove along border,
three million stained
cell clusters,

light islets, dark lobes,
thin fibrous barrier,
common enzymes

breaking down
proteins in the blood,
lipids in the chyme.

Heart

The first organ
a tentative S
enclosed in the chest,
chambers anchored
offset to the left,
apex tilted.

Complex fist,
grown figure of eight,
beating air to contract,
through lub and dub
this cone conducts.

Formed from a drop
of mother's blood,
fragment of the sun's heat
hot eye, happy diamond.

30% of all death
flows one way
in gallop rhythm,
valves pump
behind breast
between lungs,
discharging, an electric gun.

෴

Tough spiral in fine layers,
chopped or grilled on skewers,
braised then served with sauce a l'orange.

Hematocyte

You don't feel us swimming
silent as the distant tide.

We are here to be taken,
ruled out or in.

Little cargo carriages,
delivery men in uniform,
always punctual, arriving
always, leaving.

Sometimes you will see us
through the torn wall,
the sliced membrane
crusting to the touch,
flurried range of peaks,
disk of rusted mud.

Counted
named
numbered:

our multipotent defence
answering the surge, the drifting
stream's absurd roulette,

current over current
forcing us to connect.

Grand-Mary

Before I used to look
like anyone at all
there were the lips we shared
preserved in black and white.

Beneath I could discern
shades of plum and goose
cotton petticoats,
the pink of silk-lined gloves.

The nuzzle of your stare
swept me up and landed
me daily, without a thought
as I hopped two steps
a time reaching juggernaut.

When asked I would offer
we had never met,
would not, could not
couched our bond
like struck matches
in the glare.

A chapped truth
firmed over now
as I apply my lipstick
in the mirror
beneath you on my wall.

At the Sink

You look as though you are staring out to the vegetable patch, considering next year's crop, whether or not to go with the lettuce again. As the water drains you feel for any missed items, a child in a shallow bath you produce a plastic lid, rinse and place it on the rack.

Then I notice your hands in a pressurised sweep smoothing the edges of the worktop, looking for an end. Your eyes are milky and wet but they stay fixed as you rock from foot to foot, a sideways hobby horse moving through the kitchen.

At the doorway you push your hands out front, secure yourself against the frame then ripple your fingers as you heave on through and make it to the next room.

Le Café Mollien, Musée du Louvre

Located inside the best chocolate cake I ever ate
beneath Charles-Louis Müller's painted ceiling
at the end of room 77 the wife and her relative
had a ganache next to the gallery
of large-format French paintings.

You can sneak a bottle in
on the first-floor landing
where staff stand and do nothing,
even when you wave at them
a short walk from the Mona Lisa,
a pre-packaged disappointment
with a thin slice of meat and cheese.

The perfect place for lunch,
Rick recommended the patio
overlooking the Cour Napoléon
and the Carrousel Garden.
After a couple of hours of ecstasy
we agreed we needed a boost,
Glory distributing Palms and Crowns
with whipped cream set in the heart,
what I didn't expect was the warm apple tart.

This is not intended to be a great dining experience:
the space was constricted,
the young lady looked weary
surrounded by ornately carved caryatids
and bigger families with children.

Through

Taff End

Our river halves the city
like a mason splitting slate,

its fat movement pours
weir upon weir,

as bare-chested children
screech like gulls

on shingle banks
leading to green fields,

under the swaying wood
of footfall afternoons

through to ghost-lit currents
that part like legs,

beyond the openwork jetty
with candy cane poles

into the bowl closed blue.

Under the Heath

Tim says he knows of a secret
place where doctors swim
and men drive carts full
of blood and babies and legs
that will burn to ash, get sucked up
the chimney then feather
the city below.

A pair of blue swing doors gulps us
down a concrete tunnel. Hearing
the beep of traffic, we make
for vents as vermin, nooks appear, pulling
us to the walls.

We watch light grow
in flashes, a man in a green suit
and goggles moves by,
the logistics of life and death.

Regrouped we turn
into the reek of bleach
and damp and pain,
a white figure appears,
coat flapping, tie tucked
into shirt, hands at hips
making to draw pistols.

What are you doing here?

He strides towards us
taking metres as inches,
we leap trolleys of laundered sheets,
vault pallets, crash

into sacks of waste, sprint
for the finish,
           dip our heads
to meet the exit with a push.

NATO, 2014

An aria grows behind me
as I stir, sniff thyme,
meat and wine rise through
windows of white birch,
seeds fluttering.
I cover the pot,

the soprano wobbles distant
as a pulse beats over us
the fifth time this hour.
I agree to stop counting
blades, guessing the model,
the country, the guest.

Outside we stand, face
skyward, watch it circle,
ground shivering like a patient
in shock, wait for the buzz
of life to be presented to her,
the slap of defibrillator
against gravelled earth.

Earlier in the city
checkpoints emerged,
bollards rose from the earth
cameras chirruped
from branches where men
in blue caps flanked
the streets, the castle
encased and aglow.

A friend's son was cautioned
for walking, the docks clogged
full with nuclear carriers,
divers in speedboats scanned
old walls and crowds waved
as if it were a bank holiday.

The obese craft heads back east
to the golf course where tanks
patrol the ninth and steel
secures the inroads.

We return to the table,
feel floorboards shudder,
lock eyes and reach for the ladle.

Sunderland

I fly   I land   I walk   am cargo

on a train across the deep, bridge arcing
my body thrust forward like folded paper

or a leaf   a telephone un-cradled   a hook

released in a straight line hawking to the sand
near the big hotel and the empty lots, by the sea.

The Way to the Hide

To the north of here a canal runs
through the long divided county.

Where cargo swam lily pads float
large as platters, ducks move
above miniature shoals.

Along the tow path wild garlic
clusters between sleepers
serving as benches.

I think about us
feeding the birds,
imagine you crouched
in the green shade, examining
fungus, consulting the guide.

I note the woods where fallen
branches could make walking sticks,
lightsabers, swords. Hoof prints
lead to the farm but I turn
to the wetlands, for the hide.

It is perfect quiet as I tilt
into the view. A family of rabbits
twitch below. I hold my breath
for a heron.

The Way from the Hide

A dark chamber but for the slab
of light out front, face the reeds,
still my breath.

Slight movement at the lens
edge, shift my weight,
foot to foot.

Rabbits judder, young and old
muscles contract, magpie's screech
then off.

Out under canopy, lone wedding
march through sweet briar,
nodding narcissus.

Lacewing lands then flies for the lock
where a capstan squats, an old man
smokes to the water,

                    nod our good mornings,
            return to the leather of my car.

Murmuration at Manorbier

In the church porch
medieval flowers bloom
across plaster like mould.

The wooden door warns
of trapped birds that die,
when pushed it creaks
loud enough for horror.

We breathe damp air,
read notices that cling
to another era or belong
in an Archers script.

We twitch down the aisles
alert for watchful vicars,
phantoms at prayer.

Behind the nave
a dresser sits with crockery,
I picture pensioners
huddled over fig rolls
despairing of the roof fund,
the earthquake in Nepal.

Sunday school squats
in the north transept
a miniature ark,
crayoned worksheets,
a collage of eggs,
chairs kicked back from the table.

Weaving between pews,
hand-knitted kneelers show;
berries, poppies, crosses,

Sing to the Lord on a musical score,
dates marking a life,
a duck called Elizabeth,
a posy for George.

We leave holding hands,
take the steep track towards
the beach. Halfway down we pause
as the waves crash
against seaweed and shingle.

To our right a flock of starlings ignites
from the castle, we turn to face them.
Their movement beats through us,

as we watch, we sway.

Outside In

No hug, a shrug
and winter coat, it's spring
as we stand square,
white breath between us,

we slow walk through
the side door onto
a blocked floor, I recognise
lights hung high
across arcs, the gated
vestibule a weekly shop,

wooded scent
of footsteps hum
into silence

how bare it is,
this eastern inclination,
a layout that could
contain prayer mats,
a cabinet of scrolls,
papas,

how odd we are
in herd, shuffling through
domes, to sing songs
suitable for this soul.

Paris, December 25ᵗʰ
for Alex

mute winter window
two paces from bed
you watch white-white
specks bless my face

charging the spiral
as if a slide, bells
quicken our pace,
into the dizzy courtyard,
greased with life we stop,
inhale morning, step into the quiet
hall of salons past,

onto Balzac holding hands
the cinema's Chaplin
meets my gaze
and you smile
to the pigeons

on the Champs-Élysée
a surprise, casual
arrogance, throated
bustle of trade
wetting the day
a baby's head

we slip empty
into George V,
fake ivy flocking
the Givenchy front,
yellow light caught
in leaves we pull

scarves to noses,
rub elbows, chatter
of New York, Tokyo,
Trocadero, home

outside a palace
winking at the river
mulled hands cosy
brittle purchases
bagged and across
the bridge we nod
serious, a first this trip.

gendarme crackles

at the shoulder, Asian girl
in tears, backpack open
to five weather-old men
lined against railings,

under the tower
all smiles and snap
then down the ramp
to the boat,
        the water and off

Vasa

With Östermalm behind me
it could be Paris towards the water,
down the avenue May bites
skin and empties its lungs
across my neck.

Over the river hopeful
faces placard slogans
in civil uniformity.
I stop to read, forcing
my brain to meet words
I know as hints, *Europa
moderaterna!* Small
graffiti swastikas swiped
across faces, clean
roads and a harbour
that ticks like a clock.

I arrive through the park
as coaches draw to the kerb,
minute against a barbican
hanger, poles protruding
like stadium lights.

Clicking ahead of a group
I enter the vast room
to confront a wooden hulk
from a bad dream.
A door shuts and seals
the air around me timber,
new acoustics operate
from mast height down
through subterranean floors.

There is the sudden urge
to scream, ape-swing
for the crow's nest before
leaping, a cliff diver at pearls,
treasure, oblivion.

Instead I skirt the perimeter,
stern ornate with gargoyles,
crest polished like stars,
posts from a giant's bed,
rigging lashed as webs,
cake layers of gun, the hull
a pair of hips, a shallow hold,
shapes carved smooth
with meaning explained
in a circuit of panels:

proud king
        fearful court
empty stomach
        voyage told in metres
elevated central mass.

I am unsealed, turned
through into the store,
I make purchase
of a royal mug, three postcards,
a magnet. I steer my way
to the tram-stop, then check
my ballast before boarding.

Lucilia Sericata

Call the woman with old knowledge
as the Mayans did, give her your pain,
she will eat it limbless and sterile,
making hot flesh cool.

Call the ageless nurse
who will lay on your soft wound,
taking your tears for her bride
throughout the dreamtime.

She will arrive and leave,
arrive and leave,
if you call her.

An A to Z of Saints

Aloysius fired a gun
Bernadine melted sinners
Christina survived a furnace
Dunstan played the harp
Elizabeth carried roses
Finbarr rode the sea
Gengulf slept with the king
Hugh sang after death
Illtyd guarded the Grail
Jerome suffered with guilt
Kilda is an island
Lorenzo swung to tears
Margaret expired through grief
Nicholas punched heretics
Osith consolidated Essex
Paula renounced amusement
Quentin floated intact
Rita swarmed with bees
Sithney preferred mad dogs
Theodora worked in a brothel
Ulfrid broke Thor with an axe
Virgil knew of another world
Walburga caused oil to flow
Xystus died with his deacons
Yves wore a hair shirt
Zoe refused to submit to Mars

Going Feral

It comes as a red shock
across the Lino,
spattered beak litter,
feathers, a claw

then a fur pocket
of flesh playing dead,
splayed limbs,
cruel angles,

a new growl
holding me back,
paw to tail, calm
flick across threshold,
victim squeak in the yard,

I bow my head:
you raise the spade
to finish it off.

The Process

From the phone in the kitchen,
I looked out to the buttermilk yard,
gave a faceless interview,
heard the ticking of boxes
down the line
from the current family unit.

In due course a social visit,
we cracked jokes like eggs
into empty jars, faith is not funny
for workers or the state.

The training happened to us
over three bright days,
we lit the reading list
and smoked through
as phantom sheep.

Then came therapy across an empty view,
a conversation with a stranger on our lawn,
psychoanalysis without the psycho, or the analysis.

We gained take-off clearance
in a quiet room on the edge
of an orange suburb,
were sent home to wait

for three casual women
in Per Una scarves
who came with a picture,
like queens to the manger
noting our response;
The air contracted around us

then a hot flood flowed
for three long months
until we washed up at your door,
to meet your eyes,
                       our lives,
                               our ark.

Bridges I Have Known,
composed in Waterloo Gardens

Over this trickle I caught sticklebacks,
decanted them into cola bottles
not thinking to make holes for air.
In the morning I found them
belly floating, my mother
explaining suffocation.

Slicing above the Ouse winking
cameras, men in cagoules,
a suspended walkway
that pointed home,
arches to rival Brunel's.

From the top deck a lobbed apple
bouncing like a head through drizzle
down into the streaming glow
of traffic on the slip-road,
through to the never dawn.

A padlocked view, coffee
white breath and the only
flesh bared our knotted hands,
resisting the world where god
is not allowed.

On this wooden path
ladybirds teach our boy
to walk, a Labrador
spins him like a seed,

we throw pebbles to water
because poohsticks are not for the likes of us.

Out

The Way Out

is where you left it
is a pair of high-heeled boots
is a Sunday afternoon in May
is eating tomatoes with your grandmother
is not decided in a vote
is the way forward
is raining pigeons in Rome
is your children
is in the sink
is a waitress called Hazel
is taking up the flute
is a cold meat platter
is not the way out

The way out is here
The way out is the way back

Fix

This long summer
the sky grows navy,
stops before black
heat melts tarmac,
as we turn into Elm St
and see you wave
                like grass,

to a large man
on a child's bike,
topless, hard sweat
rising from frame,
eyes flutter, water
                over coral,

the delivery car
thrums to the curb,
you form a queue
before the lane
flushes out empty faces
                like wolves.

Parks

Men in tracksuits huddle, smoking
on the edges of women who share
cigarettes over pink prams.

The children who know
one another play
some distance away
near bins and long grass
where a family picnics
with a bag of crisps.

Down the road space opens,
a slide leans against its own hill.
Fathers wear ski jackets in the smoke-
free zone, mothers arrive after checking
out books from a library never marked
for closure. Each ward waits within
two metres of their primary
care giver, until it's time to sprint
for ice cream, to the van or the parlour.

Up the hill there is no queue
for the swings, our son
is the only child watching
dog walkers on the green,
runners in Lycra and quiet
gates that lead to the private
estate with its discreet place
of worship, its decent view
of the city.

Skin

        like a cliff-face, this discoloured strata,
        works deep through
        fur camouflage
        composing heat,
        barring entry
        where colonies cultivate flora
        on a pre-stretched bed,
further down
daughter cells move,
become organised junctions,
formations of mechanical strength
shedding from the surface,
blood-nourished,

        in the basement a thin sheet
        controls traffic, fibres of action
        bind growth in release,
        remodelling repair
for a cushioned landing
of elastic strength, a harbour of nerves
giving touch and heat,
sweat, glands, vessels
divided in two:

        superficial region, projecting fingers knit
        the deeper weave, root and hair and nail

below fat pads

        this covering, this guardian
        parchment that crackles.

Edgelands

There is a picture in one of those yesterday books that makes you roll your eyes. It is described as 'Children playing on a rubbish dump'. You are about six years old, smallest of a group of girls. The dump looks like a bomb site, which it probably was, or the moon, which it surely wasn't. You don't appear to be playing at all. More like you are pleading with the bully to stop, or that you have had to share bad news, or that your friend has had an idea your father wouldn't like.

Down the road they have demolished the labs to make way for flats. The council wants a fallow period before construction starts. We don't know why. The plot has grassed over and butterfly bushes bloom. You pick the buddleia 'for mummy' and clasp your grandson when he hands it over. I try not to roll my eyes.

Under the Weather

I phone to tell you it's raining where I am
three streets away, you are in the garden
where you state it's dry, cloudless
as a baby's brow, becoming warmer
as we speak.

This morning I read about a wave
of heat so bold it has been named
after a woman who is heading
for us – the inexperienced,
as we speak.

The article said we would need
to find new shade, change our routine,
swap bathrobes for walking boots,
eat biscuits instead of crackers,
even turn the way we speak.

Cathays Cemetery
for Meryl

This long cut home is stuffed
with notable Anglicans,
non-conformists,

> *boxer, politician,*
> *soldier, bishop,*

even Romans spread
flat across the bronze
winning view,

> *collier, writer,*
> *magnate, surgeon,*

loosened slabs silent
like an unlit match
the carriage porch

> *cricketer, baron,*
> *aviator, victim,*

memorials
creak at the push,
fresh beds sink,

> *mixed heiress,*
> *plantation spinster*
> *helper of the blind,*

a friend's husband,
a poem,
their children.

Asti, Balcone

The same heat over here, like breathing
through hessian folds, until the gust

of a spritz arrives on my lips
and San Secondo chimes

from the glass in my grasp.
Orange liquid spills

into view and Don Bosco
rates the drive across the clay.

A child's squeal two floors
below nods me awake

as the sky wobbles with light.
I stand and push my weight

against the metal. The thwack
and skree of movement beyond

my complex amuses *me*,
until recently a coil of bonded nylon.

I swallow the last of the syrup
and follow the cypress lines

to heaven. The opposite of prayer,
a moment filled with fact.

Tours, Jardin

Just the cat in the hot,
a rusted bistro set
on pea shingle.

Coiled lavender troughs,
the wall unweeding
like an unlaced boot.

Nodding clusters
of grass, the air a unified
ssssshhhhhh
against the pages.

A small red bug,
a plinth of bricks, gecko
poised stage left,
tongue jabbing through the heat.

Roath, Garden

In the bud, right in the heart
ripped through, peeled back
then pulled—
as though a child has been here

or, a neighbour's cat,
a feral breeze, easy
in the yard. I think of all the hunters

from end to end, birds for bats,
chasers and pouncers, spinners
and creepers looming.

From the tilt of the outhouse
the sun eats down
on the day, crosses the extension
and starts away.

St George's Castle

The old capital sits on a hill you must climb when visiting. The view from the ruins tells the island in miniature as if splayed across canvas.

On the way up artists show their impressions amongst plump bougainvillea, retired couples called Gillian and Tony pause to catch the scent along with their breath, while the lacemaker sits on a plastic chair.

Not far from the top is the café where you can eat cheese parcels made by a woman from Essex who married a local and loves it here.

Take good shoes and binoculars, for the sunset is spectacular and despite the earthquake many fig trees remain.

Port El Kantaoui

We follow the shore's curve
from one mile out batting
away yards in hotels, branded
towels on slices of beach.

Your teeth reflect the sun
and we wonder what will
appear over the rocks.

Bathers fade into distance
as we note the last guard,
black suit and tie, here
for our safety

rocks have been placed
in defence of the sea,
we remove our sandals,
size up the boulders.

You splay your toes, tree frog
scamper beneath the glow.

I press my hand against
the surface, its jagged
warmth pushes into me.

If I slip out here my head would crack,
I could twist or tear,
you are beyond as I heave
onto the mass.

We arrive in a harbour
and don't want a plate,
or a bag or a pot,
so an old man hisses,
we laugh at no joke.

In this new old film
set with excellent service,
we order drinks, a pirate ship
floats before us next to a yacht,
dock lines tickle the air.

The sun hunkers behind the medina
and a cat curls between my legs,
as you pay and stand to leave,
I ask where is best to eat.

Rumspringa at the Lake

You've been on rumspringa and you're not going back, you took off your headscarf and folded it into an origami crane, placed it on the dinner table, gave it a tap with your index finger to check she rocks.

When you called I thought you were going to say that your son had broken his leg, that your car had blown a tyre, your mother had died, or a large crack had appeared in the side of your house and a river had broken through spilling into your lounge, that a plague of mice had eaten your clothes, that you were getting an extension.

Instead, you told me that you drove down to the lake where swans nest and geese call, you spread out your cloth and sat very still listening to the sway of willow, the creak of your breath. You watched boats circle the island and traced the shadows cast by gulls overhead, you walked back to the car and released its handbrake, tapped its rear as though it were an origami crane and watched it pick up speed until it landed in an almighty splash rocking the boats and swans and geese into a thrilled chorus and then you headed up the hill, scarf in hand, folding as you went.

Mount Ainos

We spiralled the mountain
flanked by firs, insect hum.
Leant into the steepening
land like it was strong wind.

Each turn promised us silent
trees watching over cool space.

At the summit I was static
heat so my body sank
against the pylon
out of place at the peak.

We looked into the haze,
could not see Zakynthos,
Ithaca, Lefkada. We had no water,
or fruit, we each took a photo
and began our return.

Over drinks, I showed you
how ants trail towards crushed potato chips,
surprised you didn't already know.

I looked up our day and discovered
it was equivalent to climbing Ben Nevis,
or so the website said.

Signal at Banceithin

1.

Leave the cottage,
follow the path
through the wetlands
by the fire pit
onto the public road.

After the old mill
bear left, rising
for five minutes,
ten at most, past
small holdings until
you hit the fork.

Here is a good place
where you can look
back on the house,
count the sheep,
spot birds of prey.

2.

If you are lucky
you will see a lamb,
think it trapped
between fence and bank.
Stop to consider returning for help
until you notice it leans
against mother, blended
with the land, wonder
if it's feeding or asleep.

3.

Look up: you will be given
five kites hung in a dance,
slow motion marionettes
swooping against white.
A male will dive at the remark,
you have never seen so many
together at once.

4.

Take the right lane where you will find
local produce and an honesty tin.
Sometimes there is reception
outside the farm with a broken
fridge in place of a letter box.

Notes on the Poems

Hematocyte – Red Blood Cell

Lucilia Sericata – Common green bottle fly whose larvae are used for therapeutic purposes.

Rumspringa at the Lake – (In some Amish communities) Rumspringa is a period of adolescence in which boys and girls are given personal freedom ending with the choice of baptism into the church or leaving the community.

Acknowledgements

Thank you to Dr Alex for your endless love and support. Thank you to George for your existence, your love and your smile. Thank you to Professor Aneurin Jenkins for your company and your irreverence.

Thanks also to my friends and family for their support. In particular the families Briggs and Zunino for their hospitality, Victoria Radford for her incisive eye, the members of InkSplott (Mark Blayney, Zillah Bowes, Rebecca Parfitt, clare e. potter, Katherine Stansfield, Christina Thatcher, Hilary Watson and Susie Wild) for their opinions and advice. I am grateful to my students who keep me learning.

I would also like to thank the editors of the following publications in which some of these poems first appeared: *Two Thirds North*, *Orbis*, *The Lonely Crowd*, *Poetry Salzburg Review* and *Poetry Wales*.

Discover new writing with Parthian

www.parthianbooks.com